Deeply
Notched
Leaves

Deeply Notched Leaves

POEMS

Jeanne Powell

TAUREAN HORN PRESS
Petaluma, California

Manufactured in the U.S.A.
TAUREAN HORN PRESS
P.O. Box 526
Petaluma, CA 94953

ACKNOWLEDGEMENTS

Dual Face of Fear appeared in
TWO SEASONS and on a website.

Did You Know? appeared on
two websites and in TWO SEASONS.

Swing Dance appeared in
WORD DANCING (2013).

Every Indifferent Glance appeared in
TWO SEASONS (2014) and
in BUILDING SOCIALISM anthology (2020)
under different name.

Journey appeared in
CADENCES (1996), MY OWN SILENCE (2006)
and WORD DANCING (2013)

Table of Contents

special thanks to
Susan F.

I have lost my smile
but don't worry
the dandelion has it

THICH NHAT HANH

Writing Memoir is Hard

Writing memoir is hard
you knock on doors nobody wants to open
let the past stay past!
      under padlock and leafy moss blankets
you knock on those windows with tiny panes
memory won't let you in there, out of pity.
too rough on your consciousness,
emotions likely to rile up and stomp.

Writing memoir is hard
you have to go r-e-a-l-l-y slow
walk along dusty pathways with a watering can,
stop to take in deeply notched leaves,
hear the sighing of tree branches in the wind
as they recall close cousins cut down.
you go home and chant as candles glow.

You hold jars of pickled beets your grandma canned.
caress earrings blue and silver your mother left
before she walked away, and that brown radio
in an antique store just like the one your dad
listened to? you stand and whisper to it, close
your eyes and imagine, simply imagine where
he might be buried. writing memoir is hard.

A gray stone library beckons and you climb its
steep and winding staircase with urgency –
at least you did before the plague year.
you stroll along the shelves and touch book spines.
when one touches you back, you open and read.
memories slip from printed pages, rifle through
your curls, nestle in your crimson scarf.

Close to the Bay you walk the Embarcadero.
ancestors float in, waving from fishing boats
a thousand miles from Great Lakes territory.
you recall fish frys, lamps hung from trees
and laughter lighting up sundown shadows.
the tide goes out before –wait! – before
they hook a place in your memory.

On public transit, electric bus and metro car
people parade past, and you inspect for that trace
of yesterday others find in family bibles, in albums
bulging with photos posed and candid.
a stranger smiles and greets you by your birth name,
unknown out here on the west coast.
what are the archangels trying to tell you?

Start with the little girl first – you know, the one
with long braids on the cover of February Voices.
find her again. won't be easy but gain her trust
and the cadences will emerge, will outshine
manufactured dreams, break through your silence.
this memoir business is hard
but where else are you to go?

Dual Face of Fear

In my city
walking along my streets
looking like the visitor you are
you give me that look that says
you are questioning my credentials
my authenticity
my right to be here
in my city.

Walking in my direction
you suddenly notice
my golden brown roundness
and show all those attitudes
entertain all those postures
grabbing your purse
and holding it close in
as I walk past you.

Let me tell you something
all the while you brush past me
wearing African jewelry and corn-row braids
a touch of blackness in fashion where you come from
while you clutch your designer knockoff
making me unwelcome in my own 'hood
when I walk by, on my sidewalk
let me tell you something.

You clearly cannot tell the difference
between what is real and what is fake –
so listen up real good, wench.
If I wanted to, I could remove
your fake face and paste it

3

on that designer knockoff,
but since no part of you is real
why should I bother?

Two Blues in a BART Station

Words say everything.
A proper house.

A transit platform
passage
change
transition
A transit gateway
portal
voyage
journey

Women filled with today's promise
even as they bear yesterday's sorrows
passed through a turnstile one by one
suddenly imprisoned

The gaze
when they felt it
this gaze
when it crawled over them
suspended hope
belittled dignity

Such a long moment
brown faces averted
black faces shut down
once I was among those
frozen at the turnstile

This time, this moment
I was at the gate
small-sword at the ready
trained in fencing, dueling
I thundered at plantation gazes from
two tall males in blue, dressed in guns

You! Why do you gaze?
this is not your job!
six feet tall boasting guns and batons
this is not your right!
accosting innocents with badges flaring

You create an agony-column
you are here to wreak havoc
with hopes and dreams
you! No! you, stop now!
lower your eyes! leave this station!

That predatory gaze
filled with bloody intentions
Running eyes over black and brown bodies
not your privilege any more
you are on report now and forever!

Two tall cops turned red and grew small
predators dislike being called out.
this transit station is our proper house
passage through the gate is our rite
passage through is our right now!

Remembering words can say everything
I assembled an army, phrase upon phrase
with celestial help I assembled an army
to safeguard the meridians of this place
small-sword in hand, I assembled an army

I met a friend for coffee and beignets
We never spoke of this
No one needed to speak of daily battles

We crossed each bridge,
slipped through each turnstile
clothed in Spirit.

"Did You Know"?

[Fruitvale BART station,
Oakland, CA, January 1, 2009]

my country 'tis of thee
sweet land of liberty
of thee I sing

did you know before today
a bullet fired in disdain,
callous indifference
into a young father's back
as he lies face down on harsh cement
will power through, race through
his body prone
bounce off the pavement cold
and splash back into vital organs
like the heart and spirit and soul,
leaving no room for compromise,
explanation or forgiveness
and no time to say goodbye
to his lovely baby daughter?

but you know now...

of thee I sing

[For Oscar Grant]

About That Noise

New neighbors upstairs, smiles and good will
Nice to have you in the building, I say, almost
Convinced sincerity and good cheer rule their house.

You'll love it here, I say, as they move in
Bustling with boxes and lamps to light their way.
Free of any concern about their place in the world.

Moving is hard work right? On top of whatever
Else is going on in their busy well-scrubbed lives
Fresh from a world of picket fences painted white.

We grew up in the same country, right?
Not possible a small voice said, which I ignored
Until 2:00 in the morning broke with loudness.

Do they know what time it is?
Almost donned eye glasses to walk upstairs
A small voice inside whispered no, wait.

Recall one thing. You did not grow up
In the same country they did. There was a wall.
And lots of fences, remember?

And it's 2:00 AM, dark outside as you are dark.
What happens when they look out and see you?
Will they remember who you are?

No, better to endure their heedless noise
Recall these young Americans were trained
In a country very different from yours.

Endure the noise until morning, then text
The resident manager, who passes for white
So you will be safe for another day.

My Briefcase is Huge

My briefcase is huge
grins, frowns, raised brows
fascinators, chapeaux

where to put all the disguises
so neighbors and competitors
opponents and colleagues

do not sound alarm bells
when my shadow walks past,
pauses, to take in a setting sun

or the opening of a marigold.
I must hide my confidence since
they see it as "other", as not OK

for a sun-bronzed ghost
to recall an ancient past
greater than any of theirs

shape-shifting is a must
updating my arsenal as
absurdities grow rich

and futures become scarce

11

The Time That is Given

It was so much easier then, in that time when
no stars were visible and she sat under a tree,
its branches laden with pine cones, sheltered
by a green veil, safe from prying eyes.

Anemia was inevitable. No recovery expected.
wounds were too deep and too many.
sympathetic witnesses tossed food at
the base of the tree as they hurried past.

Time moved without effort, not like before
when clocks started and stopped, splattered
with blood, expectations shattered.

Celestial paperwork was examined. oh my,
these poor humans. a slight error. this one
is supposed to survive. does she need a new
body? no, the one she has will suffice.

Place guardians in the tree to ensure her recovery.
there is much more for her to learn and accomplish.
tawny owls will keep watch through the night.

Place paper and pen nearby. One day she will
discover them and realize what to do.
first, she needs time to learn to walk again
and to leave the shelter of this tree.

And twenty years later, she did.

Interrupted

denied ice cream on a summer playground
her falling-snow poem absent from school anthology
Dorsey Brothers orchestra played for white grads only
little stuff really, but a quivering grew inside

doors slammed in her face, windows barred and shuttered
successful test-taker left off the hiring list
certificate after college diploma after degree
mistaken for the parking lot attendant, the upstairs maid

that restless energy, imprisoned, began to rise
stewing, simmering until the moment fists
were clenching, fingernails slashing closed palms
she knew that blood would force a reckoning

anguish flooded her green reeds, golden rushes,
drowning in vivid bloodbursts year after year
till anger's ugly cousin began to breed – fibroids
like stalagmites, staccato highrises – blared in her womb

you have to get cut, the experts said, get cut to get safe
stem the flow, turn the tide, regain control so she took
anesthetic via spine, stood sentry while they cut away
the evidence, results of a dream deferred, hopes dismissed

here, take these little gold pills, you're so young, so pretty
we don't want that to change, do we? They didn't get –-
that potential no longer flowed, was not replaceable
warrior/woman/girlchild interrupted. Everything changed

she doctored herself from that moment, brought forth
healing words in prayers, on parchment, restaurant napkins
nightclub and city park, coffee house and church pew.
another path, she queried? Spirit flowed to light the way.

13

A Walk in the City

She stood high on city steps
Her prep school escort waiting below

Our eyes flashed recognition, she and I
We spoke as though connected from years ago

Deep Montana farmland
Michigan iron and steel

We spoke from the heart, about men
in the world we used to know

Hard work, sturdy and muscular
Remembered denim and drenching sweat

We spoke of high country in harsh sun
Furnaces of fire on midnight shift

Where are they now we wondered
Strong shoulders and those roughened hands

Deep voices and flashing eyes
Not here, we said, not in the city

Too hard to go back, we thought
In silent agreement, I walked on

Knowing Paul Bunyan and John Henry
haunted our big city dreams

Swing Dance

When you left me to go hide
in that silk-lined casket
I pulled fresh dandelions
and hid them in my coat
until the grave diggers
rested their shovels.
I scattered your lioness dandies
on the dirt covering your new home.
Near the end of my childish days
you always did travel without me.
This cemetery trick was no new game.

To see you dance once more
to that swing music you liked on the radio
when you thought no one was watching
recalling a time before husband
and kids and worries
when you worked swing shift
with all the other Rosies
then danced the night away.
To hear you laugh once more
would have been sweet.

Patchwork

needlework on grandmother's quilt
an important part of her survival kit
golden silk fibers buried in brown wool
cotton strips dyed blue and green
tablecloth scraps and church dresses

guaranteed the most textured dreams
kindred spirits felt right at home and
visited often – no surprise she woke up
with blue shadows underscoring
each brown eye

her sister did not mean to die
did not intend to drown
her mother had no intent
to leave but that car was
moving much too fast

old age caught her dad quickly
after laying in wait all those years
when he worked down, deep
down in Alabama coal mines
from the tender age of 12

Robert newly born never left
that Harlem hospital leaving their
mother with her heart in fragments
and that long black limousine
was moving much too fast

grandmother's quilt made them feel
welcome each and every night
they chose to wrap themselves
in folds of patchwork fabric
so Lydia was not alone any more.

Awaiting Hope

Each afternoon before leaving the safety
of your books and music, visual art
and garden greenery, you steel yourself,
brace for the assault you know is waiting
just beyond the door of oak and glass.

Why are you wearing a mask?
or on one of those other days,
where is your mask?

Isn't it terrible what's happening?
oh, you think it's my fault? I voted!

So sorry about Breonna.
what do you mean,
defund the police?

Oh that awful man!
but I just couldn't vote for Hillary.
you know about Deep State, right?

Head down, scarf obscuring your face,
you hurry to Sal's where everyone
recalls your name and calls out welcome
as you walk through double doors.

Zinfandel is pouring as you settle
into a favorite chair, part-time refuge
from tedious moments and pin-pointy
people. A back seat, awaiting hope.

Wearing a Poem

She woke up somewhere in
her fifth decade and decided
to start treating herself right

A hard struggle it was
yanking permission from
the many judges holding forth

Evicting them took effort
but she did it, heaving to
with pitchfork and fire

Now she could eat chocolate
as a rite and buy a latte every
day, damn the expense

Wrap mother of pearl around
her wrist and dangle seductive
earrings from her lobes

order custom arch supports
and drape long silk scarves
around her golden neck

Wear a lipstick carnelian
in color sporting the name
"Toast of New York"

Easy to understand this
alluring defiance…she carries
a poem in her eyes

The Issue Never Changes

Ok. scream, whisper, pantomime.
send smoke signals. dance up a storm.
narrate the issue on drums. no
matter – the issue is always the same.

Move over. give me some room.
I need air to breathe too. my labor
earns me a place at the table, not outside
the rear door, waiting for crumbs.

You may be taller but I am closer to
Mother Earth. You may be able to lift
that fallen tree, but I can heal the sick
and soothe a newly born child.

Your house is big. I am happy
to be guided by fireflies as I sleep
in the forest, but I can't do that if you
cut down the trees to build your house.

Your warships patrol the horizon
and you rule the high seas, but your
sailors have no food unless my
fishing boats have room to harvest.

This is your last chance to do more
than line your pockets with misbegotten
gold. storm clouds gather as icebergs
melt. can't you hear the volcanoes?

Oh, I see. Now I understand. You hear
your own screams through the smoke
and ashes. No one else can get through.

Remember Our Names

2000 years ago we lived and fought and died
You may not remember but our names are carved
in stone, in legend, in the hearts of our people.
Small and wiry, we women championed fierceness.

Was it not enough the Han invaded our nation?
We even paid taxes to those patriarchal bullies.
They raised our taxes, my husband protested
and the Han invaders had him executed.

Did they think I would retreat to a house
by the Red River and grieve in widow's weeds?
They clearly knew nothing about the sturdy women
of the Hong River delta, the crimson river.

My sister and I raised an army of 80,000
women and men, we fought this Han intrusion.
sturdy and fierce and unrelenting
we fought the invaders year after year.

Even in our defeat, the Han did not win.
My sister and I fell on our swords but
Our ghosts fed them nightmares for 900 years.
In retreat, the enemy dragged their swords.

Every Indifferent Glance

Very clear he was
about his outlook in life

Work with what you know,
work with what you have,
first-person care is the rule

Let every glance be indifferent
to others, once you are clear
they pose no threat

She was small in that alley corner
He typed her, then ignored her
with every indifferent glance

Stretching under a thin red coat,
shivering every breath she took,
so small in that corner of the alley

Not worth a serious look
in his backgammon world.

Rose where did you get?
sprinted through his memory,
quickstepping past old pain

Rose where did you get that red?
that other one had been a miniature too
in her merry-girl crimson shawl.

He shrugged and repositioned
his hard-won nonchalance
all through evening shadows,

23

so that every indifferent glance
could find this new heart quickly
in case she lasted through the night

She awoke in that alley corner
under a flowering full moon,
glanced both ways and then sat up

Beside her – a coffee mug, a whiskey cup
and poetry by Ho Chi Minh
Wide-eyed, she reached for the poems.

With gentle caution, he brought her
a red shawl, he brought her a safe welcome
He offered a chance to walk a new path

New Girl

We noticed the new girl right away
her long braids finished with ribbons
no one wears that style any more
and she doesn't smile, just stares
as though searching for something

We are the popular girls. Well,
some might say mean girls but
we never intend to be mean
some decisions we have to make
so we can remain popular

Our Penelope really is mean
when you cross her but we are
teaching her to mellow out and
when she doesn't, then we get
mean until she does, you know,

Mellow out. Back to the new girl,
Lydia by name. looks like she reads
a lot of books. those black-rimmed
glasses mean business, right?
too smart means she can't be

Popular, at least not with us, and
we are the only ones who matter.
we'll find out her secrets. Show a
little mercy to the shy ones and
they always spill their guts.

Reading Aloud

She seemed in trance
on my front porch
slender and blonde
but then one disadvantage
needing to call
my front porch her home.

She sat in the far corner,
a single book resting
on her rolling suitcase.
as I retreated up the stairs,
she read aloud to Dubliners
who used to drink with her.

Confession = no envy here
but I wonder how exactly
did she anger the Fates?
yet her dreams remain intact.
She read aloud fiercely
for all the world to hear.

Remembering Miss Canton

She carried memories of Portuguese Canton the way she styled her short hair and the shadows under her eyes – so watchful, never judging, but not forgetting. In her way she was surrounded by high walls of patient brick, her doors adorned with iron, just like Old Canton. A tiny square storefront was what she could afford in San Francisco, when she found it necessary to start a business. Not like old Canton – no face threading for demanding women on the sidewalks for her.

She painted her shop white, the walls and molding, even the floor. Her windows gleamed with pride to show off the cleanliness of her emporium, to prove she had nothing to hide. Broom and mop stood near an altar bearing incense. Tools of her trade displayed on gleaming counter, pure and untarnished. Spotless white towels, jackets, neck dusters hung in plain sight. No subterfuge. In the window a hand-lettered sign, hair cut $10. It could not be clearer. Miss Canton sat and waited, sure in the rightness of her enterprise, certain of the beauty of her path in these summer days.

Most afternoons one or two customers stood in line for a haircut or mustache upgrade. Often there would be no one waiting. I made a mental note to see if she could cut hair to my satisfaction. Many mornings Miss Canton sat quietly drinking tea, waiting for customers who were sure to come. Appointments not necessary. She sat in relaxed fashion, certain in the knowledge of her good work.

One morning she clung to a chair near a white wall, not looking up. Her shoulders sagged. I wondered on her behalf, wondered about her rent, whether she was overdue and how she was getting on.

Another day I walked in her direction and could not find Miss Canton. Her shop was no longer there. A dusty window held a grubby sign in commercial lettering, FOR LEASE.

A block away at a corner store with large windows, was a new barber emporium. Young hipsters placed plants in windows and posted a neon sign out front. Original art adorned walls brightly colored.

Their sound system piped contemporary rock through the shop. The new store had a catchy name and a presence on Facebook and Instagram. Business was very, very good.

Dearest Yvette

Dearest Yvette, it has been too long since we talked. I do telephone with regular frequency, but we don't seem to connect the way we did.

Could it be those Trimline and Princess telephones you installed on all three floors about 30 years ago? Technology has changed so much. I wish I could convince you to replace them. You always lean toward the thrifty side.

Those phones were chosen as accessories, to complement your drapes and pillow covers back in the day, when it was considered smart to imprison each room in a color scheme. Naturally you don't wish to hire a new interior decorator to rescue you from all that beige and aqua.

You asked about writing letters when we last talked, or tried to hold a conversation – I on my silver Android and you on your aqua Trimline. Yes, we used to exchange news-filled letters with great enthusiasm for 20 years. Then you abandoned your red IBM Selectric for a dull gray desktop computer and wrote less often.

I think you were focused on translating notes from journeys to the Caribbean and Africa. You planned to write a book or publish a few academic articles, but neither happened. Instead there were … interludes of mysterious silence.

That French diplomat who decorated you for contributions to French-American cultural relations – was he the reason you lost interest in writing? You still opened your postal mail back then, commenting at length on the details of my life and worth, so I felt appreciated somewhat. Never a word about him. These autumn days, you hardly ever open postal mail, which causes no end of embarrassment for you – driver's license no longer current, tax bills overdue, and memberships lapsing. This never used to be your style.

What is causing your loss of attention? I know it is not the French diplomat who courted you with ardor, since you always preferred couples, mostly in Alsace-Lorraine. We often wondered about those summers on NEA fellowships.

Lately you host fewer dinner parties and attend fewer galas. Your gossip is not nearly as interesting as before. And you seem to be in another room when we are talking. Out on the patio, upstairs, downstairs? Not sure which room you are in these days. Could it be … ? Oh my dear Yvette.

Ikea at Midnight

So she heard a guy yelling half past midnight,
just as it started to rain. Rain wasn't much,
a few drops here and there. His yelling
matched the uncertain rainfall – rush of
words, little volume, silent hesitation

He wanted to share, had information we all
needed to know, but – but no one had time
to listen. The effort it took to open drapes,
raise windows, turn down the internal noise
it was more than anyone could manage

Next to the man in the rain was a Ikea lamp
discarded by her neighbor for a newer one.
the man in the rain uprighted the lamp, adjusted
its shade and suddenly it gave him light
gave warmth and clarity to his voice

"Do you see what I'm saying, how important
It is to listen to the rain, to Mother Nature?
how important it is to shelter each other,
to not abandon hope?" raindrops intensified
his speech and upward gaze

So she heard this guy yelling as she threw her
wuzband's suits out of the window she
finally opened. "Thank you" he said. But
she could not hear the man lit by Ikea's lamp.
she was done listening to him, to anyone.

All Her Marbles

Where did they come from, she mused,
gazing at her marbles of clay, stone
and glass. Sarah opened locked cabinets
and feasted hazel eyes on her collection of
multicolored balls. Fingering micahs and
cat's eyes, she chuckled and sighed.

Of course Sarah knew the specific source
of her marble haul. She recalled
the name of each little classmate she had
neutralized in order to steal his marbles
all those years ago: Billy, Marty, Calvin,
Henry, Alvin, Bobby, Davy.

What challenged her was the lack of
specificity about original source. Marbles
graced the ashes of Pompei,
tombs in ancient Egypt, and were part
of games favored by First Nations.

During teen years Sarah labored over
her marble hoard, hiding it from kids
with no interest in aggies or alleys or
ducks, who could care less about
jaspers and bumblebees.

Sarah had her own small mansion,
a tribute to thrift and theft through
the years. At any time of the day or
night she could stand before her
collection naked and imperious.

Fired up with admiration
staring at steelies, corkscrews and
shooters, always surprised how
those hard little marvels could bring
her joy.

Her Waxy Voice

What do you think happened?

Difficult to tell really.
they did not spend much time
with the rest of us.

Just kept to themselves
more than any
other couple on the beach.

Yeah, you're right.
I would see her tending cactus flowers
in full thorny bloom
behind their bungalow

Going on and on in that
waxy voice of hers,
burbling about nature.

Right, and he spent his time
on the beach,
weaving on a portable loom,

Looking at the sea
for inspiration, and maybe
for relief, for rescue,
from her.

© 2021 Jeanne Powell

Give Me a Minute

Give me a minute. I need time to recall. It's all a jumble
right now. I downed three shots of that new tequila, the
one with three pregnant spiders at the bottle's bottom.
So a few images are fuzzy from last night in Fern Alley.

There was a big crowd, you know, everyone in costume
for All Hallows Eve, I mean Samhain, or Halloween.
A pirate sported a heavy sword on her hip and a Viking
carried a mean axe on his shoulders. That astronomer
in medieval robes flashed a mysterious globe. It glowed.

A smoke machine on the fire escape kept hissing and
filled the air with blue clouds. Be patient and I'll try to
sort out what happened. Am I the only one conscious?
Oh, two bartenders in intensive care?

Somebody dressed like Satan threw pumpkins from a
balcony. Merrymakers took exception to being pumpkin-
headed like that. Superheroes used their capes to fly up
to the balcony and made short work of those pumpkin
tossers, dropping them into a big iron cauldron.

Oh, sorry. Did not mean to get off target. You want me
to stay on topic. Please remind me, dear detectives, what
is the subject? Oh right, all those bodies clogging Fern
Alley, illegally blocking a fire lane. It was that tequila.

Oh, there was a hearse. I remember that. A guy named
Frank, a friend of Mary's, threw bodies into the hearse
and the car lurched away. Another round of spidery fire,
and well, then you all showed up. Any tequila left?

A Ring in My Ear

Been there for a month now in the middle of my good ear
a ring, not silver or gold – that would have been useful –
but no, more like a trimline phone, or an old-fashioned
kitchen timer, or that creepy film on late-night "creature
features" where something horrible wearing a mask rings a
bell and says time's up with a halitosis kind of cackle
on a cloud-filled night about an hour before the storm

What storm, you say? Well the one that always happens
after an alarm bell or a clarion call or gongs agitated
but oh, you want to know about the ring in my ear.
Well, at times I think I'm hearing a telephone in the next
apartment or a timer for the eggs I used to poach every
morning before the storm took out power

Other times it's like a doorbell from another era, when ringing
sounds were more polite and beckoned you to inquire as to
their source. Once I thought a handsome monk was circling
a copper bowl with a wooden striker, and once I thought it
was my guardian angel playing at triangles to get me out of
the doldrums.

So, doctor, I wish I could help you more.

The Kids Upstairs

They tumble down carpeted stairs
Chock full of yesterday's mischief-making
Face gems immortalized with eyelash glue

Tomorrow's stars in last stages of puppyhood
Vogueing in front of cell phone cameras
sampling tequila shots from their wet bar

Such gorgeous energy
Not clear yet on what awaits them
Sorority cubs on the cleaner side

I tolerate the noise upstairs
Because I remember

Young Dancer

Bend, rise, jump
a bad idea in
a three-floor walkup

wooden floors creak in protest
neighbors complain with
grouchy alacrity

wiser to take to the stairs
steep steps in the dark
race to the rooftop

sweep away daily dust
with a dodgy broom
take a position

nights of lunar fullness
bend and stretch
rise and glide

jump and turn
to happy exhaustion
and. then. just. Dance

You Look Delicious

You look delicious reclining on that bench
bathing in midday sunlight
soon you'll start to sweat and then
cook slowly in that spattering of sunblock
we'll have to turn you so the sun gets to roast
all of you, every muscular crevice

You look so peaceful and table-top ready
in that blue lagoon dozing under an array
of edible blossoms we sprinkled
before dedicating you to Yemaya
and pushing your raft into the water
waiting to embrace you with eagerness

You look so ready to be immortalized on canvas
posed but relaxed between peaches and pears
eggplant and cucumber across muscular midriff
grapes and cherries tracing from lips to knees
bananas placed strategically above Sunkist
oranges and tangerines

You look so happy collapsed in a snowbank
applause and laughter all around
your cross-country push was the best in show
as we pelt you with snowballs our eyes lock
anticipating long talks and hot drinks
I'm eating you with my eyes

Forget About the Shoes

Forget about the shoes
you look better barefoot, remember?
In those saucy red pumps you
teeter-totter and in your beloved stilettos,
you're the leaning tower of Pisa

All that money you spend on polish
painting fingernails and toenails
why cover them with leather?
don't get me started on those silly
friends who want you to wear pleather!

But those yellow satin slingbacks
now they were really something
you wore them when I was knighted,
remember? classier than the queen
you were that day.

I'm telling you
forget about the shoes

Blood on the Carpet

High maintenance flirt in a Vera Wang gown
he typed her from that first moment
on an ocean cruise, but her pulsating
currents of emotion drew him in,
starting with their first dirty martini.

More than once he warned himself
and thought to warn her, but never did,
let's break up before we meet. Never
happened in the summer, spring, winter or
fall. In fact he never fell so hard before.

Twenty tumultuous years in Bombay, NY
and San Francisco. Now here they were
standing in front of Parc Hotel off Union
Square, further apart than ever as they
squared off right after cocktail hour.

It was about so much more than those dirty
martinis. Why was the bellman trying on my
Pierre Cardin suits? Well, why do you need
two massages a week from those pretty
little girls? Answer me that!

Marinating in troubled silence for a moment,
they started in on each other again while the
concierge summoned a cop to stand between
them, not wanting old marital blood to spill
On the freshly laid welcome carpet.

My Gift to You

This iris
    this rose
        this daisy

        floating
    in hundreds
on a river

in France.
    airborne miracles
        clever-slip through

        a heartbeat in time.
    blossoms I place
in startled hands

creating gardens
    forever fresh
        in the soul.

inspired by Lee Mingwei's
The Moving Garden for
SF Asian Art Museum

Silence After a Sound

Silence after a sound
the one we heard or thought we heard
smart turnaround as the mind
ponders. friendly sound? a threat?
a challenge? enjoy as amusement?
be alert to a teaching moment?

Silence after a sound
a toddler laughs at grandpa's antics
then looks in awe as grandpa falls
in the garden among roses blooming.
another game, or a final exit?

Silence after a sound
he hears her scream, turns and runs,
runs toward her scream but too late.
he sits by her crumpled body
crushed by the silence.

The driver sobs apologies,
then pleads with silent body language,
seeking forgiveness without words
as sirens devastate the silence.

Is silence ever empty of sound?
there is the echo bouncing again
and again off the wall of silence
surrounding our thin mortal lives.

Silence after a sound
is red like blood escaping flesh
is blue when sunset surprises you
is golden after marigolds spill
into your fevered palms.

Immense and Silent Moon

Sipping synthetic plum wine from gourds
nibbling dried fig replicas, walking at ease
under an immense and silent moon

shifting our grenade launchers
from right shoulder to left in unison
although we were walking at ease

we listened to loudspeaker recordings
of songbirds now long extinct
for no birds sang now

any land we conquered in this realm
was subjugated without mercy
and no birds sang now

we continued to walk under
that immense and silent moon
wondering at images on wristwatch screens

tiny multi-colored flutters with names
orioles, robins, nightingales
what possible use were they

still, their odd warbling could be useful
as military code and did arouse some faint
emotion while we walked at ease

our turn to feed the bionic watch dogs
their ability to detect robots bought us time
to reflect under an immense and silent moon

Show Some Restraint

Please, I appeal to you
show some restraint
stop blaming yourself
self-flagellation and crying in public
that's so last century
no need to feel guilty
we have a pill for that now.

That truckload of acorns
never park on a hill
oh, no, stop crying
you'll exhaust your reservoir
of artificial tears.
all those dead chickens
in a surfeit of acorns.

Look, just scoop up the birds,
quick-roast them on that
giant grill next to the graveyard.
No more desperate scrounging.
A hot meal for everyone,
just this once, for everyone.

Fake News

The sky is falling!
no, wait, Chicken Little
was mistaken, just an acorn
but on her way to tell
the king, she tells others.
did she even say that?

Did the king reprimand
Henny Penny for dropping
an acorn on her little head?
You know how these
stories get out of hand
before you know it.

Until We Know More

Until we know more
I cannot, must not, am reluctant to,
am dismayed at the prospect,
will not step out of the crowd.

Cannot bring myself to take
the first step to do anything
wise or rash, inspiring or
compassionate.

After all, commitment
has the capacity to bring
disruption or conflict,
confusion or collusion,

And we just can't spare
the energy now, can we?
must we? should we?
somebody please answer

So I don't have to

Two Seasons Remain

This one now > full-on season
Good days rough nights
Sun-splashed sailing
Nights plagued with lightning
Strike when the iron flames red,
The ground is parched and sly,
While the river is underground and underfed.

Good morning!
A long hello with multitudes
Of celestine cycles, red sun, blue moons.
No rocket ship equal to the challenge,
No population worthy of rescue.
Only one season remains on the menu.

Sharpen your swords. Gird your loins.
Drink red wine from your bota bags,
For Sekhmet may yet cut short
Your one remaining season with Her blood red
Compassion

About Happiness

Never cared for happiness
sense of well-being overstated
accidents happen when one is
blithering about in a state of bliss

A question of definition perhaps
absence of pain? That's good
no enemy on the horizon
freedom from nightmares

A warm fire and a good meal
a worthwhile suitor waiting
no elections? trial by combat?
a riverbank for dancing

Otherwise, not suitable use of time
this casual wandering in pursuit.
without a hard-won fight
happiness is not worth keeping

Murder Your Coffee

Humidity arrived in Herculean terms
Assaulting sensibilities
Can you believe it
Even the corn on my cob dripped moisture

Everything in limbo
Magical thinking in reverse
Even fugitive wildlife puzzled over
the sheer wetness of things

Rain rain like in a fairy tale rain
To cleanse, purify, wash away evidence
Of makeshift excuses
And elections run like a lottery

Yesterday-friends and new-folk
Gloomy and demanding, expecting
Landslides of over-easy ideas, kindred excuses
Lines have been crossed

Vertigo lingers, takes up lodging
Sleeping arrangements no longer matter
Take a long slow look around
Murder your coffee with whiskey from now on.

Dubiety

That dubiety which furrows your brow
leaves you grubbing in the dirt of mourning
grumbling about lost pearls

That dubiety can be invited to leave
forget what I said about doubt
being housed in the lamp of mystery

Just extend the invitation with derring-do
get clear about it, first thing
get a picture in your head

Or else Dube will stake out territory
deep, deep in your liver and bring in
armchairs of mistrust and mendacity

Limits of Our Longing

You know how hard this is
Our finding you and you losing us
More often than we find you.
These worlds between finding and losing,
Between loving and leaving,
Are meant to confuse and disorient
Because that's how we learn
To recognize ourselves,
Before we can bind and couple
And coalesce toward shared existence.

You know how hard this is
Since you taught all of us so many
Time life living breathing dying transformations
Ago, and yet somehow even you lost your way,
as rain fell at a slant on moonless nights
And mirrors kept melting when you
Needed to scry. We forgave you and
Continued transforming as you forgave us,
Then singled me out as your successor,
Possessor.

We move in such big shadows.
Please don't let yourself lose me.
Across that silky ribbon of a river
Lies everything that matters.

After the Light Spring Rain

After the rain we quibbled
over the absence of plenty
such a little rain, so much drought

After the wetness transformed
our porch, diamond drops adorned
cobwebs and crevices and little else

After the light spring rain
left so much unsaid
our makeshift schemes imploded

Forget what I said when it rained
you look strong enough to cause a man
to tarry without thoughts of peach blossoms

After the rain, look over your left shoulder
he will still be there
housed within the light of becoming

After the rain, walk barefoot with care
and harvest the acts of faith
newly born from moments of doubt

© 2021 Jeanne Powell

Journey

The moment my soles touched the tarmac
I did not think of you at all. The old gang
enveloped me in sweet-tasting tavern songs
and marching chants, evoking times when walls
tumbled and dreams lived hard but high up where
all could see and gain the heart they had to have

In honor of my visit we would mourn Plum Street
conjure Canada outlaws,
celebrate Greektown excursions,
recall car treks to Nine Mile Drive along
rock-salted lanes to view Christmas miracles
in the snow. I did not think of you at all

At times a traffic signal took too long to change
and I would see your face in profile on an iced-over
sign warning of washed-out roads or detours just ahead
then friends would turn our car into an evergreen drive
where warmer faces waited to rekindle select days
as is proper on a journey of the heart

Once under the weeping willow in Louise's backyard
I thought I saw a wedge from a croquet mallet, faded
paint blending into winter grass barely exposed
but from the porch came shouts reassuring in their
heartiness that hot mulled wine was waiting and so
there was no time to think of you at all

Forgiveness

1
Perched in navy blue lace
teetering on a folding chair
she left yesterday's laughter
in careless heaps on the back porch.

2
This was Thursday, the very
first day of the rest of –
no, the new way of – no,
the very first day of forgiving.

3
Not quite sure how this
was going to work, she
prepared for complete and
utter failure on this first

4
This first day of forgiving – what?
no damning anyone to hell?
no cursing of his ancestry?
or someone's bad attitude?

5
Bayer aspirin and good red wine
stood near kleenex, and
cold wraps nestled with heating pads
on the hallway table.

6

She scribbled in cursive
on long yellow pads
the way she was taught
when outlining a plan.

7

Oh, gosh, time already
for aspirin and wine, just to
get started on this very
complicated business of

8

Forgiving. All those major hurts
and miniscule cuts
not to mention
gaping wounds gushing blood.

9

And why did it matter
so much anyway, this
forgiving business?
how could it rewrite the history

10

Of it all? Simple really,
so simple, the angels
said. They counseled
her from time to time.

11

Only recently in the last
century or two could she
actually hear them, and
their whispers rang true.

12

Love life and the gushing stops.
Love yourself and the wound heals.
Forgive the ones who harmed you
and the pain goes away.

13

But what about, but what about,
she shouted as she lit candles,
flashed incense and rang bells,
what about what they did?

14

And when was that,
and why did it happen?
what was your response,
why do you cling to it?

15

Strong wings formed circles
keeping her safe as she
stomped, then screamed,
scribbled, then whispered.

16

A long time later, but
short by angel standards,
she emerged with a big smile
lighting her face.

17

She knew it was safe to venture out.
Demons had dissolved in smoke
right in front of her while her
angels chuckled in contentment.

18
Hummingbirds perched on
sunflowers and honey bees did
their fertilizing dance.
She experienced for the first time.

19
Permanent holes were torn in
that towering border wall
of pain remembered, once
frozen solid with rage.

20
Such a beautiful light
she wants to show you
but realizes with regret
you must make this journey alone.

Trade Secrets

Are you guarding trade secrets
under that grimy tan fedora,
those smoke-filled glasses
and designer body armor?

For weeks now I've listened
to your theater-of-mind stories
hiding more than you reveal
Istanbul, Yokohama, Madrid

Never knew what was on the table
all those soul-stretching years
of never enough and still hungry.
Are you stuck on that winding path?

You know about patchwork quilts
and threads of no regret? Hope
is waiting undercover if you're willing
to relinquish all thoughts of applause.

Owning Her Name

She doesn't like people to know her name
so she simply does not use it.
To tease us, she splashes that other person
across her stories and poems,
keeping that part of her hidden and safe
from prying eyes and the truly ignorant,
of whom there are so many.

Recall that names once had a meaning.
A name told what you had accomplished
or what you did for a living, back when
earning a living meant honest work --
a cooper or cook, blacksmith or farmer,
a shepherd or singer of songs.

She hid her name back then even from
the government, which you could do
if you filed the right documents.
After a while people die or wander off
somewhere, and no one remembers
any different.

Until an archangel sent a stranger
to call out her name on a city bus
to remind her she was supposed to be
about something in her life, beyond
tap dancing in the garden and
sipping green tea in the park.

She keeps whatever undercover shreds
she can muster as she walks in the woods
and ponders what mischief she may slip into
so the world will know she is still on the job.

Are We Not

I laughed and sipped champagne
took command of the room
confidently relaxed my vigilance
and let repartee run rampant

His glance crossed the room
caught me unawares.
After flashing my eyelashes
I retreated to safer ground

 Another day I jaywalked mid-block
sure of my timing, but then I
stumbled on a concrete crevice
and went flying, caught unawares

He was there in an instant
hand on my independent elbow
rescuing me from a fall.
How did this positioning happen?

Relax, I said softly to myself.
Spirit has sent you a guardian
do not dismiss him merely
because he is handsome and young

You may be worthy of admiration
allow your genuine self to bloom
a brave and startling truth here –
are we not miraculous?

The Last Year

The thing is, the last year is never the last year.
someone or something always interferes with
your belief that eating peaches off trees and
dancing in flower gardens is done.

Try again, Fate says, and with a spill of vibrance
this time. See how your cup is half full? Recall
the old friends who look you up when they are
in town, and did you forget those Jacquie Lawson
greeting cards that pop up in your email?

You walk in the shadow of sorrow, yes.
Few pairings last for eternity, but memories
are that much sweeter. Happiness forever is
for those on the other side.

Someone may have said life is easy, but
don't believe that guy. He sells used cars at
midnight. Enjoy winter's ice and ability to
freeze pain until the warmth of spring can heal.

Bless the pain when you can; it means
you're alive and able to get back on roller skates
tinted with oak dust and lit by tiny flames,
and resume circumnavigating the world.

Haiku

clever songbirds
sing in our secret garden
romancing the sun

porcelain tea cup
sky blue springdances with white
tea leaves spill through cracks

pretty poison drips
spoiling milk, killing flowers
mother nature grieves

two Senegalese
dance in Bloomingdale's shadow
cable car bells toll

Six Word Memoirs

rent eviction
jobless affliction
California nightmare

my womb
belongs to
me exclusively

penny candies
hopscotch dandies
childhood gleaming

early death
sudden losses
lifetime grieving

blankets of
sadness remembering
ordinary days

parler queens
harlequin maybe*s
whiffin privilege

FEBRUARY VOICES (1994)

She writes…with the honesty of a survivor and the elegance of a stylist. Whether satirizing … or keening … or offering her own story with irony and gracefulness, her Voices are promising poems. I recommend that readers read them, and recommend that she write more.

— CHRISTOPHER BERNARD
EDITOR, *CAVEAT LECTOR*

CADENCES (1996)

Cadences is an impressive collection that fulfills the
promise of February Voices, drawing us into its rhythms
and meanings on many levels. These poems...sing
and rage in ways that are compelling, enchanting and
unforgettable.

– Dr. Louise M. Jefferson
Wayne State University

MY OWN SILENCE (2006)

My Own Silence is a testament against the worst type
of silence - that of indifference. These are poems
of conscience in which the poet ends her silence by
transforming her outrage into unforgettable images....
Yet, despite the world's cruelty and sorrows, the poet finds
much in which she can rejoice.... This is a book that looks
hard at life...and embraces it in all its complexity.

– Dr. Lucille Lang Day
Author of *Wild One* and *Infinities*

My Own Silence is a vibrant, cohesive collection of story-
poems, with bold beginnings and endings neatly tucked.
The writer spins dramatic filaments into poetic gold with
a rhythmic ear and a robust voice. Cousin to Whitman,
Jordan, Collins – Jeanne Powell's literary threads are
expertly woven into America's tapestry of struggle and
redemption.

– Stephen Kopel
Author of *Spritz* and *Tender Absurdities*

CAROUSEL (2014)

At a time when the confessional mode has banished American poetry to one vast self-mirroring island, the work of Jeanne Powell nudges us again and again to break out of our little selves. Whether celebrating the triumphs of Australia's champion Aboriginal athlete Cathy Freeman, berating a hellish vacation in the Sierra foothills, disclosing the subtle and not so subtle pain of social injustice, or commemorating a powerful, dancing mother reared in the big band swing era, Powell rocks. Unfailingly, the open-hearted spirit of her prose and poetry allows us to re-experience our membership in one another.

– AL YOUNG
CALIFORNIA POET LAUREATE EMERITUS

TWO SEASONS (2014)

Jeanne Powell's latest collection of poetry entitled Two Seasons must rank among her best work, either poems or essays. These poems are inspiring and inspired because of their uncanny ability to transmit genuine feelings of rage and love, justice and injustice, with an eloquence and power that few contemporary American writers can match.

Her gifted "word dancing" comes across forcefully yet gracefully in both oral recitations and on the written page. When I heard Jeanne deliver in public one of the exquisite poems from Two Seasons, I was stunned at the impact it had on the audience. Yet no one could have been more deeply moved than I because, as a professor who has often employed poetry to convey complex theories over many years, I could appreciate how, in a single poem, she managed to communicate the fierce emotional realities of the human experience.

– DENNIS DALTON
PROFESSOR EMERITUS,
POLITICAL SCIENCE / POLITICAL THEORY
BARNARD COLLEGE, COLUMBIA UNIVERSITY

About The Author

JEANNE POWELL holds degrees from WSU in Michigan and USF in California. She is an award-winning poet and essayist, with four books in print from Taurean Horn Press and Regent Press: MY OWN SILENCE, TWO SEASONS, WORD DANCING and CAROUSEL. She founded Meridien PressWorks™ which published 20 writers in 20 years. Jeanne's film reviews appear online.

For ten years Jeanne facilitated Meridien Writers, which met monthly in San Francisco. For a decade she hosted Celebration of the Word, a weekly open mic in the City. Jeanne has taught in CS, OLLI and UB programs on college campuses. She has been a featured performer in coffee houses, cafes, libraries and bookstores.

jeanne-powell.com
starkinsider.com/author/jeannep

CPSIA information can be obtained
at www.ICGtesting.com
Printed in the USA
LVHW022342090421
683918LV00002B/4

9 780931 552243